I'm the Chef!

D1336481

Shetland Library
Rosalba Gioffre

WITHDRAWN

641.5

A young chef's Italian cookbook

270074

This edition first published in the UK in 2002 by
Franklin Watts
96 Leonard Street
London EC2A 4XD

ISBN 0 7496 4650 0

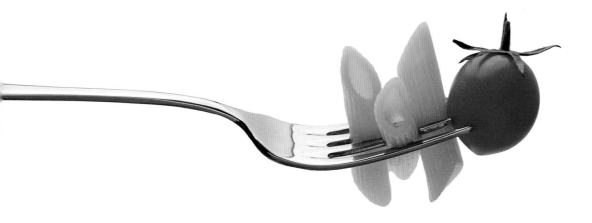

Copyright © McRae Books Srl, 2001

All rights reserved. No part of this publication may be
reproduced, stored in a retrieval system, or transmitted in any
form or by any means electronic, mechanical, photocopying,
recording or otherwise, without the prior written permission of
the publisher and copyright owner.

Project Manager: Anne McRae
Graphic Design: Marco Nardi
Photography: Marco Lanza, Walter Mericchi
Set Design: Rosalba Gioffrè
Editing: Alison Wilson
Layout and cutouts: Ornella Fassio, Adriano Nardi, Laura Ottina

Special thanks to: Mastrociliegia (Fiesole) and Dino Bartolini (Florence)
who kindly lent props for photography.

A CIP catalogue record for this book is available from the British Library.

Colour separations: Fotolito Toscana and Litocolor (Florence)
Printed and bound by Artegrafica, Verona

I'm the Chef!

A YOUNG CHEF'S
ITALIAN
COOKBOOK

Rosalba Gioffre

W
FRANKLIN WATTS
NEW YORK • LONDON • SYDNEY

SHETLAND LIBRARY

Contents

DISCLAIMER

The recipes in this book are suitable for children aged nine and above. They have all been prepared in our test kitchen by a mother of three young children and are safe for children of that age. Throughout the book, we have included tips for safety in the kitchen. However, since cooking involves the use of knives, boiling water and other potentially dangerous equipment and procedures, it is strongly recommended that an adult supervises children at all times while they are preparing the recipes in this book. The publishers and copyright owners will not accept any responsibility for accidents that may occur when children are preparing these dishes.

Introduction

Italian food is not only delicious, it is also easy to prepare. This makes it especially suitable for young chefs. In this book, there are fifteen popular recipes with step-by-step photographs. By following the instructions carefully you can surprise your friends and family with some delicious food. Each recipe also has special tips and tricks to help a young chef get it right, from the start. The central pages (22–23) focus on *Carnevale,* showing the fun, and the food, that Italian children enjoy at that time of year. So, have fun, or as they say in Italy, *Buon divertimento!*

Bruschetta

Toast with tomato and basil topping

This delicious summer snack is served all over Italy, but it is especially popular in the south where tomatoes are plentiful. The name of this dish is pronounced 'brusketta', because in Italian the letters 'ch' have a hard sound, as in the English word 'architect'.

8

Ingredients

2 thick slices of white bakery bread

2 cloves garlic, peeled

6 fresh basil leaves

2 tablespoons extra-virgin olive oil

salt and ground black pepper to taste

2 large ripe salad tomatoes

Rinse your fingertips in a little vinegar to remove the strong smell of garlic.

1 Toast two slices of bread until they are light golden brown. Rub each slice with a clove of garlic. The crispy surface of the toast will 'grate' the garlic and quickly absorb it.

Utensils

CUTTING BOARD

BREAD KNIFE

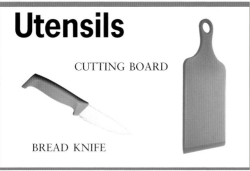

2 Rinse the tomatoes and wipe them dry with paper towels. **Chop** the tomatoes into cubes and spread them over the toast. Take special care with the knife. You do not need a very sharp one. An ordinary bread knife is fine.

TIPS & TRICKS

Bruschetta *makes a healthy after-school snack. Quantities given here will be enough for one or two. Spread the mixture on the bread just before serving so that the toast does not become soggy. Ask an adult to help when working with knives.*

3 Rinse the basil and shake lightly until dry. Use your fingertips to tear the basil into pieces and **sprinkle** it over the tomatoes. Season with a little salt.

4 **Drizzle** the *bruschetta* with olive oil to taste. If you like strong flavours, sprinkle a little black pepper over the top.

Crostini

Chicken liver toast

You may be unfamiliar with some of the ingredients in this recipe, but don't worry, the chicken livers and **anchovies** combine with the other ingredients to make a delicious topping for the toast. This dish is found all over Italy, but originally comes from Tuscany, where it is served as an *antipasto* or **starter** along with a plate of ham and salami.

Ingredients

300 g (10 oz) chicken livers, cleaned and fat removed

2 anchovies (from a can, preserved in oil)

2 tablespoons capers

salt (taste first – the anchovies and capers are already salty)

1 small onion, coarsely chopped

4 tablespoons extra-virgin olive oil

1 baguette (French stick)

TIPS & TRICKS

You will need a sharp knife to chop the chicken livers and onion. Be very careful while doing this. Hold the knife well up the handle and keep your fingers away from the blade. Ask an adult to help. Junior cooks in Italy use a half-moon chopper because they are much safer.

1 Use a bread knife with a **serrated** blade to slice the bread into rounds about 1 cm (½ in) thick. Toast lightly.

HALF-MOON
CHOPPER

CUTTING
BOARD

FOOD MILL
OR FOOD
PROCESSOR

FRYING
PAN

2 Rinse the chicken livers and **chop coarsely**. Cook in a frying pan over high heat for 1 minute. Then add the oil, onion, anchovies and capers. Cook for 3–4 minutes. Pour in 125 ml (4 fl oz) hot water, and cook for 8–10 more minutes.

3 Add salt if necessary. Remove the frying pan from the heat and put the mixture into a food processor or food mill with 2 tablespoons of warm water. Blend until creamy.

4 Spread the mixture on the toasted bread. Arrange the toast on a dish and serve.

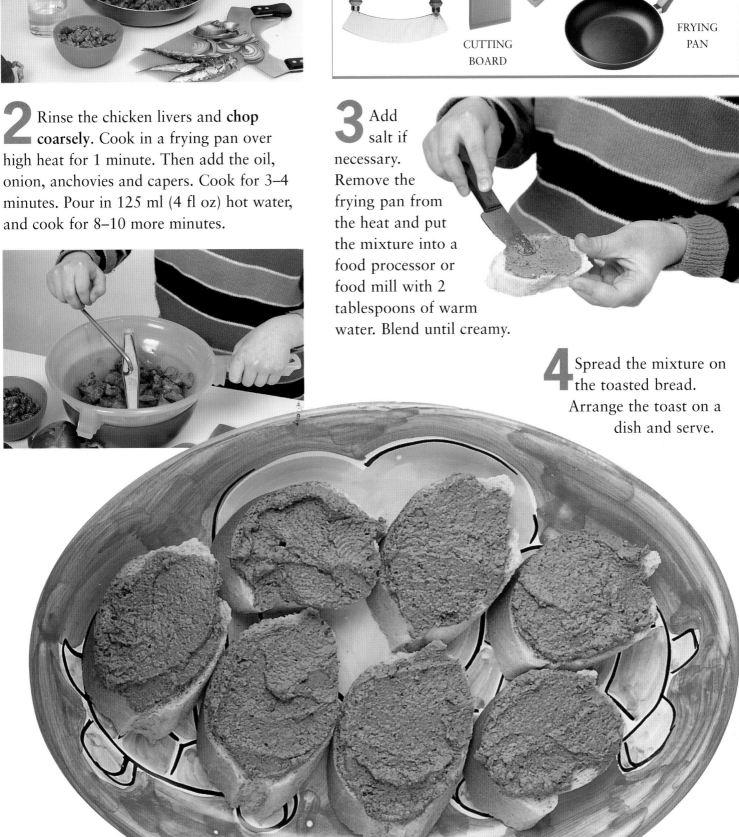

Margherita pizza

Margherita pizza

Even if you have a great pizza place in your area, try making your own at home. Making pizza is simple and fun. Two main things to remember are **kneading** the dough properly and leaving it long enough to rise. This recipe is for the classic Margherita pizza, which was invented in 1889 for Queen Margherita of Savoy. You can vary it by adding ham or mushrooms, or some of your other favourite toppings.

1 In a small bowl, **dissolve** the yeast in 30 ml (1 fl oz) of warm water, mixing well. Set the yeast aside for 15 minutes. Put the flour and salt into a large bowl.

2 Gradually work the yeast mixture into the flour. Flour your hands and use your knuckles and fists to work the dough until it is smooth and elastic.

3 Form the dough into a ball, and wrap it loosely in a clean cotton cloth. Leave it in the bowl in a warm sheltered place to rise for at least 30 minutes. Preheat the oven to 450°F (230°C/gas 7).

4 Oil a rectangular or circular pizza tray and use your fingertips to gently stretch the dough out to cover the bottom.

5 Open the can of tomatoes, pour them into a bowl and chop them. Spread them evenly over the dough. Cut the mozzarella cheese into small pieces and sprinkle it over the tomatoes.

6 Sprinkle with the oregano. Drizzle with the oil and bake in the oven for about 20 minutes.

Ingredients

400 g (14 oz) plain flour

½ teaspoon salt

cherry-sized lump baker's yeast or 1½ level tablespoons dried yeast

400 g (14 oz) can of plum tomatoes

150 g (5 oz) mozzarella cheese

2 tablespoons extra-virgin olive oil

pinch of fresh or dried oregano

Utensils

MIXING BOWLS

PIZZA TRAY

TIPS & TRICKS

Ask an adult to open the can of tomatoes and also to take the pizza out of the oven. If you do handle the hot pizza tray yourself, make sure you wear thick oven gloves to protect your hands.

Penne al pomodoro

Pasta with tomato and basil sauce

Pasta is the national dish in Italy, where it is served every day. Tomato sauce is one of the most popular toppings for pasta. Tomatoes were introduced to Italy from Mexico and Central America by Spanish explorers during the 16th century. Serve the dish with style by saying *'Buon appetito!,'* which means 'Tuck in!'

Ingredients

400 g (14 oz) can of tomatoes **OR**

500 g (1.1 lb) tomatoes

6 fresh basil leaves, torn into pieces

2 cloves garlic, peeled and chopped

500 g (1.1 lb) penne pasta

4 tablespoons extra-virgin olive oil

60 g (2 oz) grated Parmesan cheese

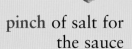
pinch of salt for the sauce

If you have some sauce left over, spoon it over a slice of toasted bread for a tasty snack.

1 Bring a large saucepan of water to the boil. Drain the canned tomatoes, put them in a separate saucepan and mash them with a fork. If fresh tomatoes are used, ask an adult to help you skin and chop them and place them in the pan.

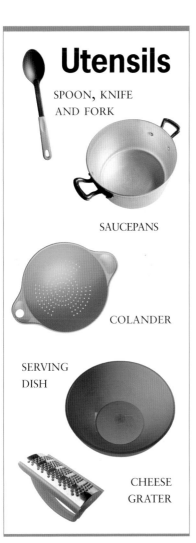

Utensils

SPOON, KNIFE
AND FORK

SAUCEPANS

COLANDER

SERVING
DISH

CHEESE
GRATER

2 Add the olive oil, garlic and salt to the tomatoes. Place the pan over a medium heat and cook for about 20 minutes, stirring often to prevent sticking. Remove from the heat and add the basil.

3 When the water in the pan is boiling, add the pasta. Cook for the amount of time shown on the packet, stirring occasionally. Drain the pasta in the colander and transfer to the serving dish.

4 Spoon the tomato sauce over the cooked pasta and mix well. Sprinkle the grated Parmesan cheese over the pasta. Serve immediately.

This sauce is good with all pasta shapes, including spaghetti, macaroni and rigatoni. You can try it with wholewheat or spinach pasta too.

TIPS & TRICKS

Be very careful when draining the pasta. The large pan of boiling water and pasta will be very heavy. Ask an adult to help you lift it. The trick with pasta is getting the cooking time right. It should be soft but still firm when you chew it. Do not cook it so much that it gets mushy and tasteless!

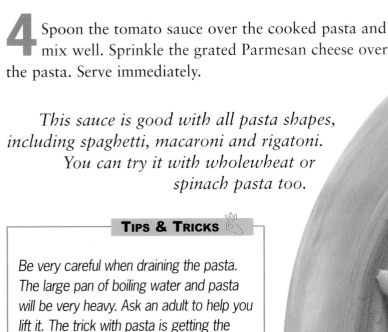

Tagliatelle

Fresh pasta with tomato sauce

Tagliatelle is a type of noodle pasta that comes from an area called Emilia-Romagna in central Italy. It should be 8 mm (⅓ in) wide. If it is wider than this it is known as *pappadelle*, and if it is thinner it is called *tagliolini*. The sauce is also a recipe from Emilia-Romagna. It features delicious Parma ham (called *prosciutto*), which is a speciality from the city of Parma in Emilia-Romagna.

Ingredients

500 g (1.1 lb) fresh *tagliatelle* pasta (or dried)

150 g (5 oz) *prosciutto* (Parma ham)

500 g (1.1 lb) fresh or canned tomatoes

125 g (4 oz) butter

pinch of salt

90 g (3 oz) Parmesan cheese

1 Bring a large saucepan of water to the boil. Put the *prosciutto* on a cutting board. Cut it first into strips and then into squares. Hold the knife firmly in one hand and keep your fingers away from the blade.

TIPS & TRICKS

Always turn the handle of pots and pans on the stove inwards so that you do not knock them. Place the large pan of boiling water for the pasta on an inner ring where it is safer.

2 Ask an adult to help you skin the tomatoes, then chop them roughly, or open a can of tomatoes and squash them in a bowl using a fork. Place the tomatoes in another saucepan, together with the *prosciutto* and the butter.

3 Mix well and cook over a medium heat for about 30 minutes. Stir occasionally with a wooden spoon. Add salt to taste.

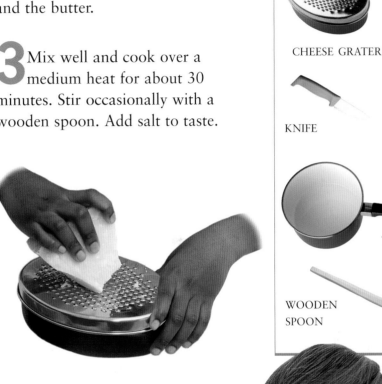

Utensils

LADLE

CHEESE GRATER

KNIFE

CUTTING BOARD

TWO LARGE SAUCEPANS

WOODEN SPOON

4 While the sauce is cooking, add the *tagliatelle* to the boiling water. Follow the instructions on the packet for the correct cooking time. Grate the Parmesan.

5 When the pasta is cooked, drain it in a colander. Transfer to a large serving dish. Ladle the tomato sauce over the top and sprinkle with the Parmesan. **Toss** well and serve.

Pasta al pesto
Pasta with basil sauce

This pasta sauce is quick and easy to make. You just have to mix the ingredients in a food processor, cook the pasta, combine the two and serve! Pesto comes from Genoa, on the Italian Riviera. Located between the mountains and the Mediterranean Sea, Genoa has a mild climate where herbs such as basil grow well.

Utensils

MIXING SPOONS

HAND HELD
FOOD PROCESSOR

CHEESE
GRATER

COLANDER

1 Bring a large saucepan of water to the boil. Separate the basil leaves from the stems. Place the leaves in a colander and rinse. Drain well and dry on a clean cloth.

2 Grate the cheeses. If you have one, use a grater with a little dish underneath so that it is easier to gather up the grated cheese.

Ingredients

30 g (1 oz)
toasted pine nuts

40 fresh basil
leaves

375 g (12 oz)
linguine pasta

pinch of salt

150 ml (5 fl oz)
extra-virgin olive
oil

1 clove
garlic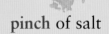

30 g (1 oz)
of both Parmesan and
Pecorino cheese

TIPS & TRICKS

When using the food processor make sure your hands are completely dry. Never put your fingers inside the processor or near the blade of a hand-held processor. To scrape the mixture off the sides of the processor, turn it off and use a spatula. Ask an adult to help you.

3 Place the basil, cheeses, pine nuts, garlic, oil and salt in a bowl and chop with a hand-held processor. If you have a food processor, place the ingredients in it and whizz everything around until the sauce is creamy.

4 When the water in the saucepan is boiling, add the pasta. Cook for the amount of time shown on the packet. Take 2 tablespoonfuls of the water from the pan and place in a serving dish. Drain the pasta in the colander and transfer to the serving dish. Pour the basil sauce over the top and toss well. Serve immediately.

Gnocchi al ragù

Potato gnocchi with meat sauce

These little potato dumplings are a favourite dish all over Italy. The 'gn' in *gnocchi* has the same pronounciation as the word 'gnome', while the 'ch' is pronounced like a 'k'. *Gnocchi* originally came from Verona, in northern Italy, where they were served with melted butter, sugar and cinnamon. In Tuscany, they are called *topini*, which means 'little mice'.

Utensils

POTATO MASHER
(ANY SORT)

MIXING BOWL

KNIFE

1 Cook the unpeeled potatoes in a large pan of boiling water. Drain and set aside. When cool, remove the skins using your fingers, then mash.

2 Dust your hands with flour and begin working the flour and salt into the mashed potatoes. Continue until the mixture is smooth and well mixed, but still soft.

Ingredients

1 kg (2.2 lb) potatoes

450 g (1 lb) plain flour

pinch of salt

400 g (14 oz) jar of Italian meat sauce

60 g (2 oz) grated Parmesan cheese

3 Take a handful of the mixture and roll it out into a long, thin sausage on a floured work surface. Cut the sausage into lengths about 2–3 cm (1 in) long. Bring a big saucepan of water to the boil.

4 Pick up each *gnocchi* in one hand and run the tines of a fork along the edges so that it has lines running around it. If this is too difficult or takes too long, leave this step out. The *gnocchi* will still taste great anyway.

5 Place the *gnocchi* on a lightly floured cloth. When the water is boiling, add the first batch of about 30 *gnocchi*. When they float up to the top, they are cooked. Scoop them out with a slotted spoon, and transfer to a serving dish. Repeat until all the *gnocchi* are cooked. Heat the meat sauce and pour over the *gnocchi*. Sprinkle with the Parmesan and serve.

TIPS & TRICKS

To avoid being splashed by boiling water, place the gnocchi on a small, lightly floured dish, dip the edge into the water, and let them slip gently into the pan.

Carnevale

Carnevale, called carnival in English, is a special holiday celebrated in many **Roman Catholic** countries before Lent. In Italy, the most important celebrations are held in the week leading up to Shrove Tuesday. After it comes Ash Wednesday and the start of the 40 days of Lent. To host an Italian *Carnevale* party, prepare the *Cenci* (this is the Tuscan name for these sweets; they are prepared all over Italy, but have different names). Encourage your friends to dress up. Make papier maché masks and paint them in bright colours. It is traditional to throw **confetti,** set off fire crackers and even to spray people with foam from cans of shaving cream! The best day to have your party is Shrove Tuesday.

This mask is one of many worn at carnival time in Venice.

Cenci

- 250 g (8 oz) plain flour
- 30 g (1 oz) softened butter
- 2 eggs
- 60 g (2 oz) sugar
- pinch of salt
- 2 tablespoons grated orange zest
- 250 ml (8 fl oz) olive oil for frying
- 60 g (2 oz) icing sugar

Sift the flour into a bowl and add the butter, eggs, sugar, salt and orange zest. Stir with a wooden spoon, then knead with your hands until the dough is smooth and elastic. Cover with a clean cloth and leave for 30 minutes. Roll out into a thin sheet and cut into rectangular strips, some of which can be tied into loose knots. Heat the oil in a deep frying pan and fry the cenci a few at a time until they are golden brown. Ask an adult to help you. Remove them with a slotted spoon and drain on paper towels. Sprinkle with the icing sugar and serve at once.

There are many costumes you can wear at carnival time. In the past, people wore masks so they could poke fun at their rulers without fear of being recognized or punished for it.

These people are celebrating Carnevale in Piazza San Marco in the northern Italian city of Venice. Carnevale in Venice has become so famous that people from all over the world visit at this time.

Traditionally, boys wore brightly coloured Harlequin costumes, such as this one. Harlequin (Arlecchino in Italian,) was a well known comic character in Italian theatre in the 16th and 17th centuries. Girls often dressed up as fairies. Today, both boys and girls wear costumes based on their favourite films or TV programmes.

Risotto

Parmesan and saffron risotto

Rice was introduced to Western Europe by **Arab** invaders during the **Middle Ages.** Risotto was invented in the northern Italian city of Milan, where it is still a classic dish. This is a good way to prepare rice because it cooks slowly, absorbing the flavours of all the other ingredients. **Saffron** adds a touch of colour, turning the rice red or gold, depending on how much you add.

1 Chop the onion coarsely using a half-moon chopper or knife. In a large saucepan, **sauté** the onion in half the butter until it is golden.

TIPS & TRICKS

In Italy, it is traditional to add wine to the risotto as it cooks. This improves the taste and, since the alcohol evaporates, is still suitable for children. If you do not wish to use wine, just leave it out.

Ingredients

1 medium onion

60 g (2 oz) butter

400 g (14 oz) rice (preferably Italian Arborio rice)

60 ml (2 fl oz) dry white wine (optional)

1 litre (1¾ pints) chicken stock, made with boiling water and 1 stock cube

1 packet saffron

90 g (3 oz) grated Parmesan cheese

2 Add the rice to the saucepan and stir constantly over a medium heat for about 2 minutes. Hold the saucepan firmly by the handle while stirring. The rice should swell and be lightly toasted.

25

Utensils

HALF-MOON CHOPPER

LADLE

CHEESE GRATER ANY SORT

CUTTING BOARD

WOODEN SPOON

LARGE SAUCEPAN

3 If using the wine, pour it into the saucepan and stir until it has evaporated. Dissolve the chicken stock cube in the hot water. Begin adding the stock to the rice a ladleful at a time, stirring as it is absorbed by the rice.

4 Continue cooking and gradually adding more stock for about 20 minutes. Stir all the time so that the rice does not stick to the pan. Taste the rice after about 15 minutes to see if it is cooked. It should be soft, but firm or '*al dente*', which means 'firm to the bite'.

5 When the rice is cooked, remove from the heat and stir in the remaining butter.

6 Add the saffron and mix well so that the rice is evenly coloured. Finally, stir in the Parmesan and serve.

Polpette al pomodoro

Meatballs with tomato sauce

These meatballs will become one of your favourite dishes. The bread swells during cooking, making them soft as well as tasty. You can eat them with a fork and finish them fast. The mixture is also fun to make because you can do it all with your hands. You can squeeze the soft ground meat together with the other ingredients and then form it into balls.

2 Grate the cheese and bread together into a large bowl. Keep your fingertips away from the grater.

1 Combine the tomato puree, salt and oil in a large saucepan. Cook over a low heat for about 15 minutes, stirring often.

Utensils

GRATER

DEEP FRYING PAN

3 Combine the mince with the bread, cheese, eggs, salt and pepper in a large mixing bowl. Mix well with your hands. Add a ladleful of the tomato sauce and stir it in with a spoon. Let the mixture cool.

4 Rinse your hands in cold water to stop the mixture from sticking to them. Use your hands to form the mixture into smooth round balls about the size of large plums. Repeat this step until there is no more mixture left. Place the meatballs on a plate.

5 Add the meatballs carefully to the tomato sauce, one at a time. Cook them in the sauce over a low heat for 20–30 minutes without stirring. Shake the pan very gently from time to time. Serve the meatballs with pasta or rice.

Ingredients

1.5 litres (2½ pints) tomato purée

60 ml (2 fl oz) extra-virgin olive oil

500 g (1.1 lb) minced beef

1 loaf white bread

3 eggs

250 g (8 oz) grated Parmesan cheese

pinch of black pepper

TIPS & TRICKS

Add the meat balls to the sauce very gently so that they don't break or splash sauce on you. A good way to do this is to dip a tablespoon into cold water and use it to pick up each meatball and then slip it into the pan.

Cotolette alla milanese

Milanese-style veal escalopes

This dish is also called Viennese **cutlets** or *Wiener schnitzel,* and some people think it was first made in Austria. Food historians in Italy have found letters that prove it was actually invented in Milan, over 1,000 years ago! These **veal** escalopes are tasty and fast to make. You can serve them with French fries and a green salad for a complete family meal.

1 Break the eggs into a small bowl, add a pinch of salt and beat for 2–3 minutes with a fork.

2 Dry the escalopes with paper towels. Then sprinkle lightly with salt on both sides.

TIPS & TRICKS

Boiling oil is very hot and can cause painful burns. Ask an adult to help you fry the escalopes. If a little oil splashes from the pan onto your hands, run them under cold water. Try to buy escalopes that have already been trimmed of fat. For vegetarians, use the same method to cook slices of aubergine.

Ingredients

2 eggs

pinch of salt

4 veal escalopes

150 g (5 oz) dry bread crumbs

250 ml (8 fl oz) olive oil for frying

3 Dip the escalopes one at a time into the bowl of beaten egg. Make sure that every part of the meat is covered with egg. Let the extra egg drip back into the bowl as you lift the meat out.

4 Spread the bread crumbs out on a dish. Lay each escalope in the bread crumbs and press down. Turn over and repeat. Shake off any extra bread crumbs.

Utensils

SLOTTED SPATULA

LARGE FRYING PAN

5 Heat the oil in the frying pan. Add the escalopes, one or two at a time. Make sure they do not overlap. Cook until a deep golden crust forms. Then turn over to cook the other side. Remove from the pan and drain on paper towels. Serve warm.

Pesce finto

False fish

This dish tastes good even if you don't normally like fish. The strong flavour of the fish is softened a little by the potatoes and mayonnaise. It is also fun to make because you can mould the fish mixture with your hands, to create the shape of a fish. Garnish your fish with the mayonnaise, adding the mouth, gills, scales and tail.

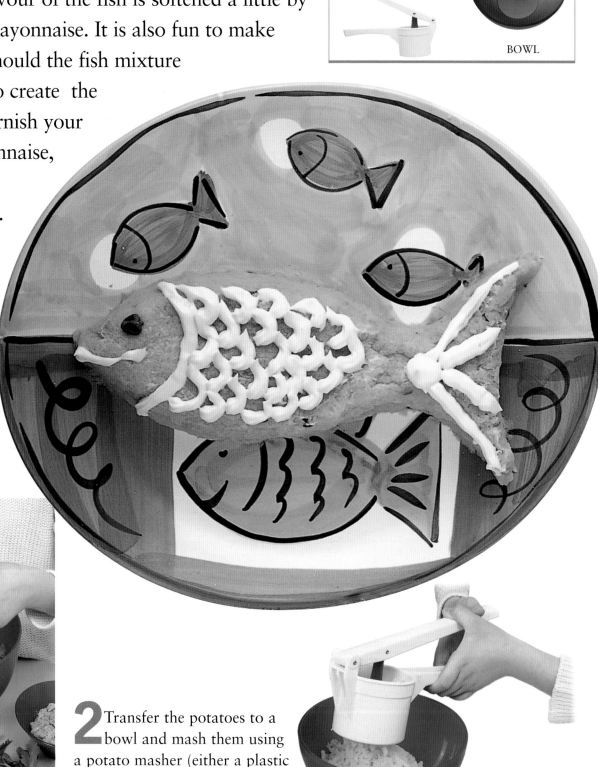

Utensils

COLANDER

POTATO MASHER

BOWL

1 Boil the potatoes in a pan of salted water for about 25 minutes or until tender. Drain in a colander. When they have cooled a little, use your fingers to peel off the skins.

2 Transfer the potatoes to a bowl and mash them using a potato masher (either a plastic one like the one shown here, or a simple wire masher).

Ingredients

750 g (1½ lb) potatoes

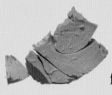
2 tablespoons finely chopped parsley

200 g (7 oz) canned tuna, flaked with a fork

125 g (4 oz) mayonnaise, in a tube

pinch of salt

1 clove garlic, finely chopped

3 Add the tuna, garlic and parsley to the bowl with the potatoes. Mix well. Season with salt to taste.

4 Turn the mixture out on a large serving dish. You can use your hands to mould the mixture into the shape of a fish.

TIPS & TRICKS

Ask an adult to help you move the pan of boiling water when draining the potatoes. Keep the tube of mayonnaise in the fridge until you use it. Cold mayonnaise is easier to draw with.

5 Decorate the fish with the mayonnaise, squirting it out of the tube. Be creative by using a little parsley to add the fish's eye. You can draw in the gills, fins and scales too.

Torta al cioccolato

Chocolate cake

If you get cravings for chocolate, this is the perfect recipe for you! When eaten in moderate quantities chocolate is not bad for you. It is not even true that it will give you spots. The latest research shows that chocolate is a mood enhancer, which means that it makes you feel good. So do not feel guilty about loving this cake!

1 Place a large saucepan of water over a medium heat. Put the chocolate and butter in a smaller pan and place it in the larger one. Stir the mixture until it is melted.

Ingredients

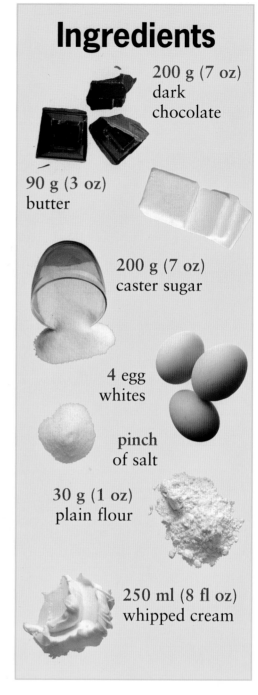

200 g (7 oz) dark chocolate

90 g (3 oz) butter

200 g (7 oz) caster sugar

4 egg whites

pinch of salt

30 g (1 oz) plain flour

250 ml (8 fl oz) whipped cream

TIPS & TRICKS

Place the cake on the middle rack in the oven. Don't open the door during the first 20 minutes of cooking time, or your cake may go flat. Ask an adult to take the cake out of the oven. Ask an adult to help you separate the egg yolks from the whites.

2 Remove the saucepan from the heat. Add the sugar and stir until it has **dissolved.** Gradually add the flour, stirring until well mixed. Set aside to cool.

3 Beat the egg whites until stiff using a hand beater or an electric mixer. Add a pinch of salt before you begin so that the eggs stiffen quickly.

4 When the chocolate mixture is **lukewarm**, carefully mix in the egg whites. Use a spatula to gently blend in the egg whites.

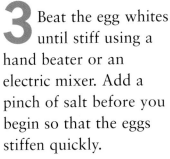

5 Grease and flour a 24-cm (10-in) diameter cake tin and pour the mixture into it. Bake in a preheated oven at 300°F (150°C/gas 2) for about 25 minutes. The cake should have a light crust but still be soft inside. To test if the cake is cooked, poke a skewer into the middle. If it comes out clean the cake is ready. Remove from the oven and turn out on a wire rack to cool.

6 When the cake is cool, decorate it with the whipped cream. (You can use a piping bag or a spray can.)

Tiramisù

Tiramisu

This dessert is so good that four different Italian regions – Lombardy, Emilia-Romagna, Veneto and Tuscany – all claim to have invented it! It is fun to make and tasty to eat. When you serve it, your friends and family will think you are a gourmet chef. The name of this dessert is pronounced with the accent on the last syllable and means 'pick me up'.

TIPS & TRICKS

If your local supermarket or Italian food shop does not have mascarpone cheese, you can use the same quantity of cream cheese instead. This dessert needs at least two hours to chill in the fridge, so remember to start early. If you do not like the taste of coffee, replace it with the same quantity of raspberry syrup.

Ingredients

5 eggs, separated

150 g (5 oz) sugar

500 g (1.1 lb) mascarpone cheese

about 30 sponge fingers (preferably Italian *savoiardi*)

250 ml (9 fl oz) strong black coffee

200 g (7 oz) dark chocolate, grated

15 g (½ oz) unsweetened cocoa powder

Utensils

ELECTRIC WHISK

MIXING BOWLS

SPATULA

8 Put the cocoa in a sieve and sift evenly over the top to finish. Place in the fridge for at least two hours before serving.

1 Use the spatula to beat the egg yolks and sugar until they are creamy and light in colour.

2 Stir in the mascarpone a little at a time and mix well. In a separate bowl, beat the egg whites until they form a stiff mixture.

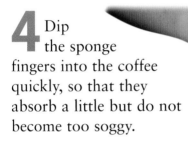

3 Carefully stir the beaten egg whites into the egg yolk and cheese mixture.

4 Dip the sponge fingers into the coffee quickly, so that they absorb a little but do not become too soggy.

5 Cover the bottom of a serving dish with a layer of the cream. Then add a layer of sponge fingers.

6 Use the spatula to spread the cream in an even layer.

7 Cover with another layer of cream and sprinkle with a little chocolate. Repeat until all the sponge fingers and cream have been used up.

Gelato di crema con salsa al cioccolato

Ice cream with chocolate sauce

Ice cream with hot chocolate sauce is one of the most delicious ways to finish a meal. Some believe ice cream originated in China, around 3,000 BC. The ancient Chinese mixed snow with fruit and honey. As Europeans came into contact with the East, the secrets of making ice cream travelled to Europe. The technique of making smoother ice cream was perfected in Sicily in the 1500s, and was exported as *gelato*.

TIPS & TRICKS

If you do not have an ice cream maker, place the creamy mixture in a freezer-proof bowl and put it in the freezer. After two hours stir quickly and put it back in the freezer. Repeat twice.

1 In a mixing bowl, beat the egg yolks and the sugar with a whisk until they are pale and creamy.

Utensils

WHISK

MIXING SPOON

SMALL SAUCEPAN

SAUCEPAN

ICE CREAM MAKER

Ingredients

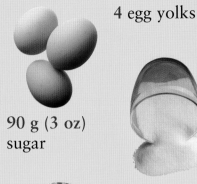

4 egg yolks

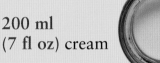

90 g (3 oz)
sugar

250 ml
(8 fl oz) milk

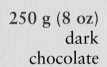

200 ml
(7 fl oz) cream

250 g (8 oz)
dark
chocolate

30 g (1 oz)
butter

2 Add the milk and then half the cream gradually, beating all the time until they have been completely absorbed by the mixture.

3 Pour the mixture into the ice cream maker and follow the instructions to make the ice cream. If you do not have an ice cream maker see the Tips & Tricks box for instructions on how to make ice cream by hand.

4 When the ice cream is ready, place the chocolate, butter and remaining cream in a small saucepan. Put the small saucepan inside a larger one half full of water and place over a medium heat until the ingredients have all melted together. Put the ice cream in a serving bowl and pour the chocolate sauce over the top.

SHETLAND LIBRARY

Glossary

anchovies small fish, often salted and dried.

Arabs a native or inhabitant of Arabia, an area located between the Red Sea and the Persian Gulf.

baguette baked bread formed in the shape of a long stick.

beat to mix a liquid or soft paste rapidly.

capers unopened buds of a flower grown in the Mediterranean area. They are often preserved in brine or salt.

chill to refrigerate, but not to freeze.

chop to cut into tiny, fine pieces using a knife or food processor.

coarsely chopped to cut in larger pieces, not in a fine, smooth texture.

confetti small pieces of paper, thrown in the air at festive events.

cutlets a flat ball of minced food, such as fish, or vegetables.

drizzle to let something fall in fine drops or a fine stream.

dice to cut food into tiny cubes using a knife.

dissolve when a solid ingredient melts into a liquid.

grease to coat a pan with oil or melted butter.

grate to cut foods into small, thin pieces by rubbing them against a grater.

knead the act of mixing and smoothing out dough before it is baked.

lukewarm something that is moderately warm.

Middle Ages the period in European history between the late 5th century and the 1400s.

mix to combine ingredients in a bowl.

pasta a preparation of thin unleavened dough, processed in many forms, such as spaghetti.

pinch measuring an ingredient by the amount held in the tips of two fingers.

rise when dough swells or puffs up

from the action of yeast.

Roman Catholic a member of the Catholic Church, which is led by the Pope.

saffron the orange stigma of a crocus flower used for colouring and flavouring food.

sauté to fry food lightly in oil over a medium heat.

serrated having a grooved edge.

sift to separate and retain the coarse parts of flour with a sifter.

sponge fingers known in Italy as 'savoiardi'. They are sweet, dried sponge cakes.

sprinkle to scatter in separate drops.

starter a small amount of a food or drink served at the beginning of a meal.

toss to throw lightly without force, within the dish or bowl.

veal the meat from a calf.

whisk a utensil used to whip food.

Index